Third Grade Homework

Real-Life Activities that Turn Homework into Family Fun

Written by Vicky Shiotsu

Illustrated by Ann Iosa

Edited by Mary Pat Ferraro

Project Managed by Sue Lewis

Project Directed by Carolea Williams

Table of Contents

Introduction

Third-grade children are eager and ready to learn. These enthusiastic young students enjoy age-appropriate homework assignments that provide successful learning experiences. When homework is fun and meaningful, it lays the foundation for good work habits in later years. Furthermore, positive homework, or "homeplay," helps establish the home-school connection and involves parents as partners in their child's daily learning experiences.

Third Grade Homework

- includes creative activities that transform homework into "homeplay"—a positive, exciting, and creative experience for third-grade students.

- provides ready-to-use reproducibles requiring almost no teacher preparation time.

- empowers parents with information and practical ideas they can implement easily as they become partners in their child's education.

- gives the whole family the opportunity to be part of the homework process.

- describes techniques that parents can use to help their children establish the good work habits essential for successful learning.

- offers teachers a choice in how to present homework to their students, giving them flexibility to tailor the methods to meet their students' needs.

Types of Homework Activities

Design your own homework program by choosing from the following types of activities included in *Third Grade Homework*.

Monthly Calendars

Twelve monthly calendars with five learning activities per week are provided. Parents and children can complete a specific number of activities each week and then complete a response journal designed for the month. A blank calendar is also provided so you can design your own activities.

Monthly Celebrations

Activities following a seasonal theme are provided for each month of the year. Invite parents and students to complete a monthly celebration and then return a record of the celebration to school.

Across the Curriculum

Engaging homework activities are presented for language arts, math, science, social studies, music, art, and physical education. Easy-to-follow directions lead children and parents through each step in the activity. Send these activities home to correlate with a current topic of study or a thematic unit.

Fun With Literature

A variety of activities are included to stimulate children's interest in books. Send the pages home for independent study or use the activities to supplement your classroom literature program.

Family Adventures

Family adventures are designed for students and their entire families to enjoy. Families are invited to experience both real and imaginary adventures. Several suggestions are offered for each adventure so children and parents can choose how they will complete the homework.

Timely Tips Newsletters

The reproducible newsletters provide parents with information to help make their child's learning experience at home even more productive. Topics include homework tips, reading, television-viewing, learning on the go, and building a child's self-confidence. Send the newsletters home throughout the year with your regular classroom newsletter to keep parents informed.

Monthly Calendars

Monthly Calendars provide real-life activity ideas for parents to do with their children. Many take only minutes to do and require easy-to-find items from around the house.

To begin, fill in the number of activities you expect students to complete each week. Duplicate the calendar and the response journal page for the month; staple them together for each child. Send them home on the first school day of each month.

Ask students to return their calendars and response journals on the last school day of the month. After you receive them, review the response journals to evaluate which activities you'd like to include in future plans.

A blank calendar at the end of this section (page 30) invites you to customize a month-full of learning to meet your students' needs. You might even want to create a month's calendar of activities for a particular child or group of children.

The July and August calendars can be used for summer homework or for year-round schools.

Choose at least _____ activities to complete each week. Check the box in the lower right corner of each calendar square as your child completes the activity. Turn in the calendar and the response journal on the last school day of September.

September

Monday	Tuesday	Wednesday	Thursday	Friday
List three things you hope to do in school this year.	Practice introducing yourself to a new student. Role-play with someone at home.	Draw a map showing the route you take from your home to school.	Write a menu for a nutritious school lunch.	Figure out the year you will graduate from high school.
Look in a phone book. Count how many people have the same last name as you do.	Write as many words as you can using only the letters in your name.	Write the full names of your grandparents. Use your best handwriting.	Draw yourself in your favorite school outfit.	Stand outside. List five things you hear.
List all the people in your family in alphabetical order.	Draw a picture using just straight lines.	Make a yummy sandwich. Then write the recipe for it.	Write a prediction for tomorrow's weather. Check how accurate you were.	Find an interesting word in the dictionary. Use it some time during the day.
Make a card telling why your family is special.	Help someone at home today. Do a chore you've never tried before.	Put a carrot and an apple in a sink full of water. What happens? Why?	Look in the newspaper. Circle the names of eight countries.	List at least five numbers whose digits add up to 7. (25, 133)
Glue leaves, nuts, and other fall items onto cardboard to make a collage.	Fall and autumn are synonyms. List five more pairs of synonyms.	Calculate how many days it will be until your next birthday.	Teach your family a game or song you learned at school.	Visit a library. List four things you can borrow.

September Response Journal

Help your child complete this page. Turn in this journal along with the calendar on the last school day of September.

Student

1. My favorite activity was _____.

   I liked it because _____

   _____.

2. The most challenging activity was _____

   because _____

   _____.

3. I learned _____

   _____.

Parent

1. I learned _____.

2. The activity I most enjoyed doing with my child was _____

   _____.

3. The activity I helped my child with most was _____

   _____.

Parent's Signature _____

Name _____

Choose at least _____ activities to complete each week. Check the box in the lower right corner of each calendar square as your child completes the activity. Turn in the calendar and the response journal on the last school day of October.

October

Monday	Tuesday	Wednesday	Thursday	Friday
Make a list of fun things your family could do that don't cost any money.	Look around your home for five things made of plastic. List them.	How many drops of water will sit on a penny? Use an eyedropper to check.	Add up the ages of the people in your family. Find the difference between the oldest and the youngest.	List one way you used each of your five senses today.
Look in the Yellow Pages. Circle three restaurants you'd like to try.	Cut a magazine picture into ten pieces. Then put it back together.	Add to this pattern: 1, 4, 3, 6, 5, _, _, _. Now write your own pattern.	Ask someone to help you practice your spelling words.	Write at least ten words that begin with a vowel.
Glue paper shapes together to make an animal.	List ten items in your home that have numbers on them.	See how long it takes for you to say the alphabet backwards. Try this three times.	Find three things in your home that dissolve in water.	Practice reading a poem aloud. Then read it to your family.
List as many planets as you can from memory.	Estimate the length and width of your bedroom. Check your guess.	Draw five different ways you could make a dollar with coins.	Tell someone at home about a book you enjoyed reading.	Draw a picture that would make an interesting Halloween sticker.
Make a funny mask from a paper plate.	Sketch a costume that would be fun to wear to a costume party.	Write a poem using as many "sound words" as you can. (bang, screech)	Count the number of seeds there are in a small pumpkin or apple.	List words that rhyme with trick and treat. Which list is longer?

8

October Response Journal

Help your child complete this page. Turn in this journal along with the calendar on the last school day of October.

Student

1. My favorite activity was _____.

   I liked it because _____

   _____.

2. The most challenging activity was _____

   because _____

   _____.

3. I learned _____

   _____.

Parent

1. I learned _____.

2. The activity I most enjoyed doing with my child was _____

   _____.

3. The activity I helped my child with most was _____

   _____.

Parent's Signature _____

Name _____

Choose at least _____ activities to complete each week. Check the box in the lower right corner of each calendar square as your child completes the activity. Turn in the calendar and the response journal on the last school day of November.

 # November

Monday	Tuesday	Wednesday	Thursday	Friday
Write the names of ten classmates. List them in alphabetical order.	Find out today's high and low temperatures. Calculate the difference.	Measure the distance from your bedroom door to the front door of your home.	Clean a closet.	Look at a grocery store flyer. List items that will total approximately $5.00.
Draw pictures of the fruits and vegetables you eat this week.	Trace around a ruler and other flat objects. Ask someone to identify them.	Design a book jacket for one of your favorite stories.	List five objects in your home that are transparent.	Describe today's weather. Tell as much as you can.
Communicate to your family for five minutes without speaking.	List three books you'd recommend to children your age.	*November* has eight letters. Write three other words that have eight letters.	Draw six symmetrical shapes.	Keep track of the different ways you use your hands today. Write them down.
Write three things you could do to keep from catching a cold.	Make a poster showing ways different animals prepare for winter.	Write a sentence in which each word begins with a different letter.	Go to your favorite spot in your home. Read for 20 minutes.	*Thanksgiving* is a compound word. List ten compound words.
Suppose you could have anyone over for dinner. Draw the person you would invite.	List each family member's special qualities. Include yourself.	Write the menu for your Thanksgiving dinner.	Ask each family member what he or she is thankful for.	Count how many days it will be until the new year.

November Response Journal

Help your child complete this page. Turn in this journal along with the calendar on the last school day of November.

Student

1. My favorite activity was _____ .

   I liked it because _____

   _____ .

2. The most challenging activity was _____

   because _____

   _____ .

3. I learned _____

   _____ .

Parent

1. I learned _____ .

2. The activity I most enjoyed doing with my child was _____

   _____ .

3. The activity I helped my child with most was _____

   _____ .

Parent's Signature _____

Name _____

Choose at least _____ activities to complete each week. Check the box in the lower right corner of each calendar square as your child completes the activity. Turn in the calendar and the response journal on the last school day of December.

 # December

Monday	Tuesday	Wednesday	Thursday	Friday
Draw a snowy scene. Spread glue on the snow and sprinkle on salt.	Read a book about a holiday in December.	Press a fork against an ice cube for one minute. What happens?	Imagine that the electricity is off. Draw six things that will not work.	Recycle a container by making a toy out of it.
Help plan the grocery list for this week.	List three ways you keep warm in the winter.	Read the label on a food can. Write three things you learned.	Ask ten people to name their favorite season. Graph the results.	In two minutes, list as many words as you can that rhyme with *snow*.
Look in this week's mail. Collect the different kinds of stamps you find.	Read a book with a family member. Take turns reading aloud.	Find the birthplaces of your parents and grandparents on a map.	Draw one beautiful thing you see in winter.	Design an award for a family member who has worked hard this year.
Write a letter to a relative or friend. Wish the person a happy holiday.	Write three things you have always wondered about.	Draw a postage stamp that celebrates winter.	Count how many aunts, uncles, and cousins you have.	Write directions for making a snowman.
Make gift tags. Tape them onto your holiday presents.	Write five phrases that describe winter.	Design a winter outfit for yourself.	List four winter activities you enjoy. What equipment do you need for each?	Make a banner saying good-bye to the old year.

December Response Journal

Help your child complete this page. Turn in this journal along with the calendar on the last school day of December.

Student

1. My favorite activity was _____.

   I liked it because _____

   _____.

2. The most challenging activity was _____

   because _____

   _____.

3. I learned _____

   _____.

Parent

1. I learned _____.

2. The activity I most enjoyed doing with my child was _____

   _____.

3. The activity I helped my child with most was _____

   _____.

Parent's Signature _____

Name _____

Choose at least _____ activities to complete each week. Check the box in the lower right corner of each calendar square as your child completes the activity. Turn in the calendar and the response journal on the last school day of January.

January

Monday	Tuesday	Wednesday	Thursday	Friday
Write three things you hope to improve on this year.	Staple pages to make an autograph book. Ask friends to sign it.	Find out the temperatures of your refrigerator and freezer.	Find three places on a map or globe you could go in January to get away from the cold.	Make a poster or book showing at least six animals that live in the Arctic.
Look in a magazine or a newspaper. Circle ten nouns (person, place, or thing).	Draw a new cartoon character for a TV show. Describe it.	Make a word search puzzle using your spelling words.	Fold a paper in fourths. Unfold it. Write a math problem in each section. Solve the problems.	Write a note that can be read by holding it up to a mirror.
Make a poster showing different ways people have fun in winter.	Draw a picture showing what your home looks like in the winter.	List five things in your home that give off heat.	Glue toothpicks onto a sheet of paper to make an interesting design.	Look at a map of your state. Write five cities you see.
Choose a sentence from a newspaper. Rewrite it as a question.	List five ways you use water in the home.	Where does your family shop for groceries? Write why you shop there.	Write a sentence using only words that begin with sh, ch, th, and wh.	Make up a math problem that involves your family.
List six things in your home that were made in other countries.	Look in a book. Find ten words with prefixes and ten with suffixes.	Put an object in a paper bag. Give clues. Have someone guess the object.	Draw an invention that would help students with their homework.	Roll a pair of dice. Add the numbers. Keep rolling until you reach 100.

January Response Journal

Help your child complete this page. Turn in this journal along with the calendar on the last school day of January.

Student

1. My favorite activity was _____ .

   I liked it because _____

   _____ .

2. The most challenging activity was _____

   because _____

   _____ .

3. I learned _____

   _____ .

Parent

1. I learned _____ .

2. The activity I most enjoyed doing with my child was _____

   _____ .

3. The activity I helped my child with most was _____

   _____ .

Parent's Signature _____

Name _____

Choose at least _____ activities to complete each week. Check the box in the lower right corner of each calendar square as your child completes the activity. Turn in the calendar and the response journal on the last school day of February.

 # February

Monday	Tuesday	Wednesday	Thursday	Friday
Find out who was president when your parents were your age.	List four qualities a person needs to be a good president.	Would you like to be president one day? Explain your answer.	List the presidents who are on the $1, $5, $10, and $20 bills.	Write a tongue twister. Say the tongue twister five times fast.
Make a picture chart showing fruits and vegetables that are red.	Cut out a paper heart. On it, write an activity that is good for your heart.	Create an animal by gluing paper hearts together.	Write a valentine note and tape it to the refrigerator for your family.	Do a kind deed for someone.
Write why you need to take care of baby teeth even though they will fall out.	Write about what you think you'll be doing when you are 25 years old.	Send a thank-you note to your dentist for caring for your teeth.	Write the full name of each family member. Circle the longest name.	Soak a tarnished penny in a cup of vinegar for 30 minutes. What happens?
List three things you do well.	Print your name. Turn each letter into a cartoon.	Research a famous person. Write three facts you learned.	In one minute, list as many kinds of birds as you can.	Draw what you might look like as an adult.
Estimate how many times heads will come up if you flip a penny 50 times. Try it.	Write a sentence or draw a picture with your eyes closed.	Draw a curved line. Figure out a way to measure its length.	Look in a newspaper. Circle ten words that have silent letters.	How many community workers did you see this week? List them.

February Response Journal

Help your child complete this page. Turn in this journal along with the calendar on the last school day of February.

Student

1. My favorite activity was _____ .

   I liked it because _____

   _____ .

2. The most challenging activity was _____

   because _____

   _____ .

3. I learned _____

   _____

Parent

1. I learned _____ .

2. The activity I most enjoyed doing with my child was _____

   _____ .

3. The activity I helped my child with most was _____

   _____ .

Parent's Signature _____

Name _____

Choose at least _____ activities to complete each week. Check the box in the lower right corner of each calendar square as your child completes the activity. Turn in the calendar and the response journal on the last school day of March.

 # March

Monday	Tuesday	Wednesday	Thursday	Friday
Go out on a windy day. Figure out from which direction the wind is blowing.	Design a colorful paper kite. Try to fly it.	Ask an adult to help you find out how far you can jump.	Give your community a new name. Explain your choice.	Mix blue and yellow paint. See how many shades of green you can make.
Visit the library. Find two fiction and two nonfiction books about animals.	Make a picture chart showing at least eight different kinds of insects.	Use a stamp pad to make thumbprints on paper. Turn each one into a bug.	Look in a newspaper or magazine. Circle ten interesting verbs.	Ask your parents what they liked to play as children. Write what they said.
If you were a zoologist, which animal would you study and why?	Circle six items on a grocery bill. Add up the prices.	Read a folktale from another country.	Begin with 100. Count backwards by fives.	Write the names of three authors who illustrate their own books.
Add to this word train: be**d**, **d**og, **g**oat, **t**in, _, _, _, _, _, _, _.	Sit quietly. List some things in your body that are moving.	Arrange cereal pieces into a pattern. Then eat your work!	Make a sketch of an interesting place in your community.	Finish this sentence in three different ways: *Spring brings* _____.
Do some spring cleaning around your home.	Make a list of five household chores that need to be done each week.	Create a musical instrument from scrap materials. Show how it works.	List ten words that have more than one meaning.	Make a stick puppet of your favorite story character.

March Response Journal

Help your child complete this page. Turn in this journal along with the calendar on the last school day of March.

Student

1. My favorite activity was _____ .

   I liked it because _____

   _____ .

2. The most challenging activity was _____

   because _____

   _____ .

3. I learned _____

   _____ .

Parent

1. I learned _____ .

2. The activity I most enjoyed doing with my child was _____

   _____ .

3. The activity I helped my child with most was _____

   _____ .

Parent's Signature _____

Name _____

Choose at least _____ activities to complete each week. Check the box in the lower right corner of each calendar square as your child completes the activity. Turn in the calendar and the response journal on the last school day of April.

  # April

Monday	Tuesday	Wednesday	Thursday	Friday
Read a riddle book. Share some of the riddles with your family.	Make a dot-to-dot picture that a kindergartner might like to do. Give it to your teacher.	Rewrite the ending to a fairy tale.	How much water do you get from one cup of ice cubes? Experiment to find out.	How many times can you bounce a ball in a minute? Try to improve your record.
Write three new uses for a hula hoop.	List five animals and the names of their babies: cat-kitten seal-pup	Make a list of rules that every student in your school should follow.	Collect different seeds. Glue them to cardboard. Label them.	Write three ways that you and a tree are alike.
Look in a cookbook for a recipe that looks good. Try it with an adult.	Play charades with a family member.	Listen to a recording of a song. Make up actions to go with the words.	Choose a story. Draw a comic strip showing your favorite part.	Act out a commercial for your favorite TV show.
What book would you like to see turned into a movie? Write why.	Make a poster showing how people can take care of the earth.	What is your favorite store? Design a flyer advertising it.	Do something to make your home more beautiful.	Make a chart listing the helpful and harmful effects of rain.
Find five new words in a library book. Write their meanings.	Draw a fancy spring hat for yourself.	Write four things you think people will do differently 400 years from now.	Make a paper airplane. Measure how far it flies. Do several trials.	List the places you went to this week besides home and school.

April Response Journal

Help your child complete this page. Turn in this journal along with the calendar on the last school day of April.

Student

1. My favorite activity was _____ .

   I liked it because _____

   _____ .

2. The most challenging activity was _____

   because _____

   _____ .

3. I learned _____

   _____ .

Parent

1. I learned _____ .

2. The activity I most enjoyed doing with my child was _____

   _____ .

3. The activity I helped my child with most was _____

   _____ .

Parent's Signature _____

Name _____

Choose at least _____ activities to complete each week. Check the box in the lower right corner of each calendar square as your child completes the activity. Turn in the calendar and the response journal on the last school day of May.

May

Monday	Tuesday	Wednesday	Thursday	Friday
Write words or phrases to describe your favorite flower.	Find a flower with an even number of petals and one with an odd number.	Look in the phone book. List two places that sell garden supplies.	Play catch with a partner. Use something other than a ball.	Read a book outdoors on a sunny day.
Cut out a magazine picture. List adjectives that describe it.	Glue tissue paper onto a clear plastic lid. Hang with ribbon by a window.	What is one book that children all over the world would like? Write why.	Read a book about nature. Tell your family about the book.	Decorate a sheet of colored paper to make a place mat for your mother.
Go outside and count how many kinds of bugs you see.	Examine a leaf with a magnifying glass. Draw what you see.	Write a sentence containing a plural, a contraction, and an adjective.	What would you plant in a garden? Draw seed packets to show your answer.	Write three creative uses for a rubber band.
Collect six things you think will sparkle in the sun. Test your guess.	Design a vehicle that would take you around the world, over land and sea.	Look in a dictionary. List the different meanings for *spring*.	Make a toy boat that can really float. Use scrap materials.	*May* has only three letters. List other three-letter words.
If you mailed three letters across town, how much would the stamps cost?	Write two things an animal does better than you and two things you do better.	Create a story character who is your age. Describe that person.	Look at the sports section in a newspaper. Circle the names of five sports.	Write the name of a sport. List the skills you need to play that sport.

May Response Journal

Help your child complete this page. Turn in this journal along with the calendar on the last school day of May.

Student

1. My favorite activity was _____ .

   I liked it because _____

   _____ .

2. The most challenging activity was _____

   because _____

   _____ .

3. I learned _____

   _____ .

Parent

1. I learned _____ .

2. The activity I most enjoyed doing with my child was _____

   _____ .

3. The activity I helped my child with most was _____

   _____ .

Parent's Signature _____

Choose at least _____ activities to complete each week. Check the box in the lower right corner of each calendar square as your child completes the activity. Turn in the calendar and the response journal on the last school day of June.

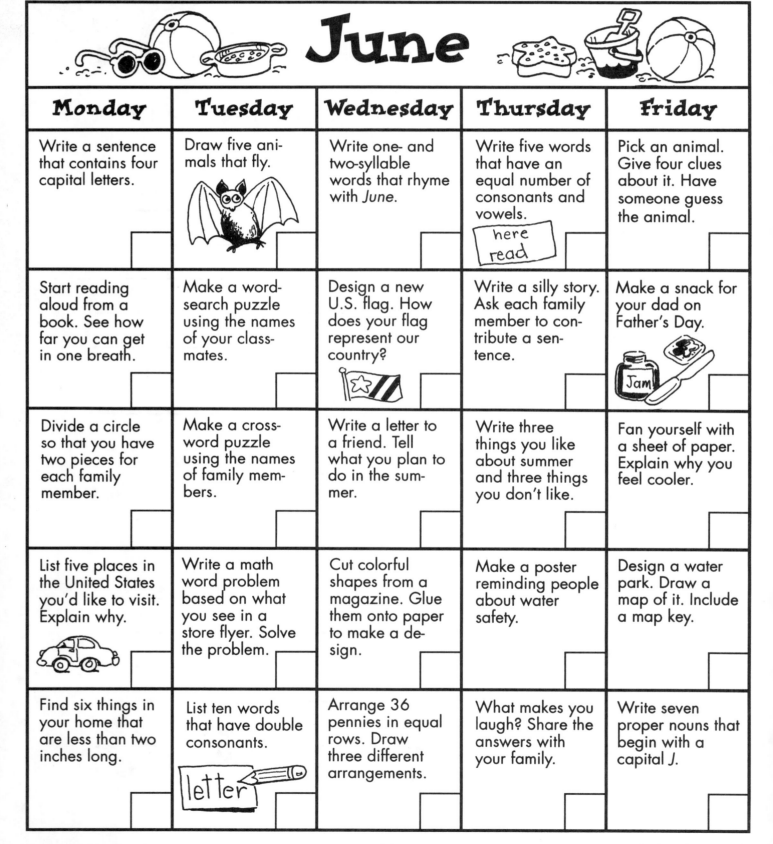

June

Monday	Tuesday	Wednesday	Thursday	Friday
Write a sentence that contains four capital letters.	Draw five animals that fly.	Write one- and two-syllable words that rhyme with *June*.	Write five words that have an equal number of consonants and vowels. here read	Pick an animal. Give four clues about it. Have someone guess the animal.
Start reading aloud from a book. See how far you can get in one breath.	Make a word-search puzzle using the names of your classmates.	Design a new U.S. flag. How does your flag represent our country?	Write a silly story. Ask each family member to contribute a sentence.	Make a snack for your dad on Father's Day. Jam
Divide a circle so that you have two pieces for each family member.	Make a cross-word puzzle using the names of family members.	Write a letter to a friend. Tell what you plan to do in the summer.	Write three things you like about summer and three things you don't like.	Fan yourself with a sheet of paper. Explain why you feel cooler.
List five places in the United States you'd like to visit. Explain why.	Write a math word problem based on what you see in a store flyer. Solve the problem.	Cut colorful shapes from a magazine. Glue them onto paper to make a design.	Make a poster reminding people about water safety.	Design a water park. Draw a map of it. Include a map key.
Find six things in your home that are less than two inches long.	List ten words that have double consonants. letter	Arrange 36 pennies in equal rows. Draw three different arrangements.	What makes you laugh? Share the answers with your family.	Write seven proper nouns that begin with a capital *J*.

June Response Journal

Help your child complete this page. Turn in this journal along with the calendar on the last school day of June.

Student

1. My favorite activity was _____ .

   I liked it because _____

   _____ .

2. The most challenging activity was _____

   because _____

   _____ .

3. I learned _____

   _____ .

Parent

1. I learned _____ .

2. The activity I most enjoyed doing with my child was _____

   _____ .

3. The activity I helped my child with most was _____

   _____ .

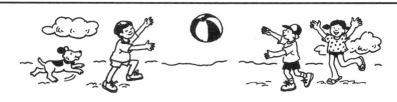

Parent's Signature _____

Name _____

Choose at least _____ activities to complete each week. Check the box in the lower right corner of each calendar square as your child completes the activity. Turn in the calendar and the response journal on the last school day of July.

July

Monday	Tuesday	Wednesday	Thursday	Friday
Make a paper badge for America's birthday. Wear it on July the Fourth.	The United States declared independence from Britain in 1776. How long ago was that?	List the birthdays of five countries.	Read a newspaper article that tells about July the Fourth activities.	Play shadow tag in the sun.
Draw yourself keeping cool in the summer.	Make a crossword puzzle with summer words.	Suppose you made a new friend. List three things you'd tell him/her about yourself.	Look around your home. List foods and spices that begin with s.	Go out at night for several nights. Draw what the moon looks like each night.
Make a graph showing today's high temperatures for five cities.	Make a map of your neighborhood. Mark three interesting places.	Look at a map. List three countries that lie along the equator.	Glue buttons and other small items to cardboard to "write" your name.	Cut a comic strip apart. See if you can put it back together.
Look at the return address on a letter. Find the city on a map.	Memorize a short poem. Recite it to your family.	Put two ice cubes in two different places. Which one melts first? Why?	Make a picture with "hot" colors (yellow, red, orange).	Mom reads the same forwards and backwards. Write three other palindromes.
Find a recipe for lemonade. Make some with the help of an adult.	Draw a maze. Challenge someone to try it.	Make up a math problem about today's temperature.	Read a book in a cool place today.	Design a fun hat that will protect you from the sun.

July Response Journal

Help your child complete this page. Turn in this journal along with the calendar on the last school day of July.

Student

1. My favorite activity was _____.

   I liked it because _____

   _____.

2. The most challenging activity was _____

   because _____

   _____.

3. I learned _____

   _____.

Parent

1. I learned _____.

2. The activity I most enjoyed doing with my child was _____

   _____.

3. The activity I helped my child with most was _____

   _____.

Parent's Signature _____

Choose at least _____ activities to complete each week. Check the box in the lower right corner of each calendar square as your child completes the activity. Turn in the calendar and the response journal on the last school day of August.

August

Monday	Tuesday	Wednesday	Thursday	Friday
Write six words that contain *au*. Saucer	Look in the Yellow Pages. Circle two travel agencies in your area.	Ask each family member to share what he or she thinks is a perfect vacation spot.	Look in an atlas. Name six cities that are located near water.	Design a pair of colorful sun-glasses.
Make up a dance in which you imitate something in nature.	Draw four things people might wear in hot weather.	List five inventions that help keep people safe.	Write directions for getting from your home to the nearest library.	Read a book with a friend or family member.
Write three problems you can solve faster without a calcula-tor than with one.	Make a poster reminding people to protect them-selves from the sun.	Count how many glasses of water you drink in a day.	Create a recipe for a cool sum-mer treat. Make the treat and serve it to your family.	Share a joke book with some-one.
Tell an adult what time it is. Do this six times today.	What's the per-fect summer meal? Draw a picture of it.	Make up a fun game to keep you cool.	Look in a grocery store flyer. Count how many kinds of fruits you see.	Look at signs while traveling. Find all the letters of the alphabet.
Draw a picture in sand or dirt. Use a stick for a "pencil."	Invent a new use for a straw.	Arrange ten books in alphabetical order according to the author's last name.	Write a math problem that has your address as the answer.	Make a postcard of where you live. Write about the illustration on the back.

August Response Journal

Help your child complete this page. Turn in this journal along with the calendar on the last school day of August.

Student

1. My favorite activity was _____.

   I liked it because _____

   _____.

2. The most challenging activity was _____

   because _____

   _____.

3. I learned _____

   _____.

Parent

1. I learned _____.

2. The activity I most enjoyed doing with my child was _____

   _____.

3. The activity I helped my child with most was _____

   _____.

Parent's Signature _____

29   Creative Teaching Press, Inc.

Monday	Tuesday	Wednesday	Thursday	Friday

- -

To the teacher: Use this calendar for any month. Write your own activities.

Monthly Celebrations

Monthly Celebrations homework offers students the opportunity to learn while celebrating seasonal themes and holidays. These easy, fun activities don't take much time, but parents will find that it's time well spent with their children.

Send home the Monthly Celebrations homework at the beginning of the month. The homework includes two simple activity choices for children to complete alone or with family members. Ask children to complete one activity any time during the month. Encourage parents to help as needed.

At the end of each activity, students are asked to write about their experience at the bottom of the page. Students may write their response on their own or with help from their parents. Children should return the homework page on the last school day of the month. You may choose to have various projects returned to school for display in the classroom.

You can use the July and August Homework Celebrations for summer homework or in year-round schools. Page 44 includes two more general family celebrations that can be used at any time during the year.

Choose one activity. When it is completed, have your child write his or her reaction to the experience at the bottom of the page. Return this page on the last school day of September.

1. School Days

Interview a parent and find out what school was like when he or she was your age. Here are some questions you might ask:

- Where did you go to school?
- What subjects did you study?
- What did you play at recess?
- What did you like best about school?
- What did you like least about school?

Write a report about your findings. Include a photo or drawing of your parent as a child.

2. A Harvest of Apples

Go to the grocery store. Buy at least three types of apples. When you return home, make a picture poster including the name of the apples and how they vary in shape, size, and color. Try the apples you bought and add a description of their taste to the poster.

Alternative: Instead of buying the apples, write the names of the various types of apples for sale and describe their appearance.

Tell about the activity you chose. What did you like about it?

_____

_____

_____

Parent's Signature _____

Choose one activity. When it is completed, have your child write his or her reaction to the experience at the bottom of the page. Return this page on the last school day of October.

1. Fall Collage

Walk around the neighborhood and collect leaves, nuts, flowers, seeds, and other fall items. At home, place the flowers and leaves between heavy books and leave them there for a week. Afterwards, glue the items to a sturdy paper plate. Let the glue dry. Then punch a hole at the top of the plate. Thread a piece of yarn through the hole and tie the ends to make a loop. Display your creation.

2. Costume Fun

Look around your home for things you could use to make an interesting costume. Use old clothing, scraps of fabric, colored paper, cardboard, and other materials to make clothes and props. Draw a picture of yourself wearing the costume or ask an adult to take a photo of you.

Tell about the activity you chose. What did you like about it?

_____

_____

_____

Parent's Signature _____

Choose one activity. When it is completed, have your child write his or her reaction to the experience at the bottom of the page. Return this page on the last school day of November.

1. Honoring Veterans

Discuss with your family the purpose of the U.S. armed forces. Talk about how the people who served in the armed forces have helped our country. Then write a letter thanking veterans for their service. Look in a phone book for the location of a nearby veterans' organization. Then deliver or mail your letter.

2. Thanksgiving Day Place Mat

Make a Thanksgiving Day place mat for each member of your family. For each place mat, punch holes along both ends of a sheet of construction paper. Thread two or three pieces of yarn through each hole and tie them together to make a fringe. Draw lines or glue on paper strips to make a border alongside the holes. In the middle of the place mats, write a sentence telling why you are thankful for the various people in your family.

Tell about the activity you chose. What did you like about it?

_____

_____

_____

Parent's Signature _____

Choose one activity. When it is completed, have your child write his or her reaction to the experience at the bottom of the page. Return this page on the last school day of December.

1. Textured Snowflakes

Make three snowflakes, each different from the others. Follow these instructions for each snowflake:

Glue three craft sticks together. When the glue is dry, tie a 12-inch length of yarn around the middle of the sticks. Tie the yarn ends together to form a loop for hanging. Decorate the sticks by gluing on small items such as macaroni, popcorn, beads, sequins and foam packing chips. If you like, glue some tinsel in the middle of the snowflake.

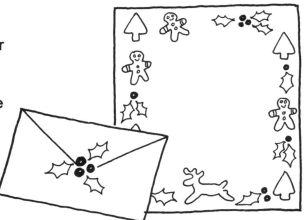

2. Winter Stationery

Collect magazines, catalogs, greeting cards, wrapping paper, or other paper items with winter themes. Cut out small pictures of things that remind you of winter or a winter holiday. Glue the shapes around a sheet of white paper to make a colorful border. Use the paper to write a letter to a relative or friend. Place the letter in an envelope and seal it. Then glue one or more of the pictures on the back of the envelope.

Tell about the activity you chose. What did you like about it?

_____

_____

_____

Parent's Signature _____

Choose one activity. When it is completed, have your child write his or her reaction to the experience at the bottom of the page. Return this page on the last school day of January.

1. Goals for the New Year

Talk with your family about individual and family goals for the new year. Write the suggestions on a sheet of paper. Next, blow up some balloons and knot the ends. Use a permanent marker to write one of your family's goals on each balloon. Tape the balloons in your home.

2. Marshmallow Snowman

This jolly snowman is fun to make in any season! "Glue" three large white marshmallows together with white frosting. Poke two toothpicks into the sides of the middle marshmallow for arms. Insert three small marshmallows for each arm. Use the frosting to attach raisins or small candies to make the snowman's face and buttons. Make a hat by rolling paper into a cylinder and gluing the ends together. Glue the cylinder onto a paper circle and use white frosting to attach the hat on the snowman. Afterwards, write a story about your snowman.

Tell about the activity you chose. What did you like about it?

_____

_____

_____

Parent's Signature _____

Name _____

Choose one activity. When it is completed, have your child write his or her reaction to the experience at the bottom of the page. Return this page on the last school day of February.

1. A Lacy Valentine

Cut a 9" circle from white paper. Fold the paper in half three times. Keep it folded. Draw half heart shapes along the folded sides. Draw a whole heart at the top edge or at the center point of the paper. Cut out the shapes. Unfold the circle. Glue the white paper on top of a 9" circle cut from red paper. Write a valentine message to your family on the back of the red paper.

2. Stand-Up President Report

Fold a $4\frac{1}{2}$" x 12" piece of light-colored construction paper in half to make two $4\frac{1}{2}$" x 6" sections. Unfold. Measure one inch from each side of the fold and draw a line. On the top half of the paper draw or glue on a picture of a president. Rotate the paper so that the president's picture is upside down. On the top, write three things the president accomplished. Fold along the lines and glue the top edges of the paper together so that your report stands up.

Tell about the activity you chose. What did you like about it?

_____

_____

_____

Parent's Signature _____

Choose one activity. When it is completed, have your child write his or her reaction to the experience at the bottom of the page. Return this page on the last school day of March.

1. Think Green

Plan a fun Saint Patrick's Day meal with your family. Prepare different foods and drinks that are green. Make place mats, napkin rings, or place cards from green paper. Add party decorations such as balloons, crepe paper streamers, and banners. When everything is ready, have everyone wear something green to the meal.

2. Wind-Catcher

Make a wind-catcher that helps you tell which direction the wind is blowing. Glue a $4\frac{1}{2}$" x 6" piece of construction paper over a toilet paper tube. Decorate with stickers or markers. Punch two holes at one end of the tube and tie on a length of yarn for a handle. Tape several 1" x 15" strips of tissue paper at the other end. Go outside with your wind-catcher. See which direction the wind is blowing by watching the tissue paper streamers.

Tell about the activity you chose. What did you like about it?

_____

_____

_____

Parent's Signature _____

Choose one activity. When it is completed, have your child write his or her reaction to the experience at the bottom of the page. Return this page on the last school day of April.

1. A Spring Haiku

Fold a 12" x 18" sheet of light-colored construction paper in half. Unfold the paper. On the left-hand side of the paper, draw a spring scene. On the right-hand side of the paper, write a haiku about spring. A haiku is a three-line poem that describes nature. The first line has five syllables, the second line has seven syllables, and the third line has five syllables. Later, read your poem to your family.

Spring rain falls gently,
Bathing the thirsty flowers
That wait patiently.

2. A Bean Planter

Glue craft sticks around the outside of a clean, empty can. Wrap two rubber bands around the can to secure the sticks. Soak two or three bean seeds in a cup of water overnight. The next day, place soil in the can. Plant the seeds in the soil and add a little water. Place the can in a sunny location and keep the soil damp. Watch your seeds grow!

Tell about the activity you chose. What did you like about it?

_____

_____

_____

Parent's Signature _____

Choose one activity. When it is completed, have your child write his or her reaction to the experience at the bottom of the page. Return this page on the last school day of May.

1. May Day Basket

Cut a 7" circle from construction paper. Fold the circle into fourths. Cut out paper flowers from various paper scraps. Glue a green paper strip or pipe cleaner stem on the back of each one. Arrange the flowers inside the pockets of the folded circle and glue them in place. Tape a loop of ribbon inside the circle for a handle. Staple or tape the sides of the basket shut.

2. Message Holder for Mom

This handy gift will let your mom keep pencils and paper nearby for quickly jotting down phone messages. Cover a clean can with colored paper. Draw designs or glue on paper shapes. Attach a clothespin to the top of the can. Put two pencils and small sheets of paper in the can. Place the message holder near the phone for your mom to use.

Tell about the activity you chose. What did you like about it?

_____

_____

_____

Parent's Signature _____

Choose one activity. When it is completed, have your child write his or her reaction to the experience at the bottom of the page. Return this page on the last school day of June.

1. A Card for Dad

Make this special card for Father's Day. Cut out a tie shape about six inches long from colored paper. Decorate the tie by gluing on pieces of colored paper. Glue the tie on a rectangular piece of paper. Write *To Dad* at the top of the paper and *You're Tie-rrific!* at the bottom. On the back of the card, write three reasons why your dad is terrific.

2. Graphing Daylight

Look in the weather section of the newspaper every day for one week and write the times for sunrise and sunset. Calculate the amount of daylight (in minutes) for each day. Then make a bar graph showing your results. Be sure to include a title and appropriate labels for the graph. Glue the graph onto a larger paper background. Draw symbols of summer along the edges of the paper.

Alternative: Check the weather section of the newspaper one day each week. Graph weekly findings over two or three months.

Tell about the activity you chose. What did you like about it?

_____

_____

_____

Parent's Signature _____

Name _____

Choose one activity. When it is completed, have your child write his or her reaction to the experience at the bottom of the page. Return this page on the last school day of July.

1. Colorful Fireworks

Color a sheet of drawing paper with various crayon colors. Press hard to make the colors as bright as possible. Then completely cover your design with a layer of black crayon. Next, scratch away the black using a pointed object, such as a knitting needle, hairpin, or paper clip. As you scratch, the bright colors underneath the black will show. Scratch curved strokes to form beautiful streams of fireworks!

2. Fun-in-the-Sun Cups and Straws

Gather a foam or plastic cup and a straw for each member of your family. Decorate the cups with stickers and markers. Make decorative straws by cutting from colored paper a sun, beach ball, or other object that reminds you of summer. Cut a small slit at the top and bottom of the paper figure. Insert the straw through the slits. Use the cups and straws to serve a cool summer drink to your family.

Tell about the activity you chose. What did you like about it?

_____

_____

_____

Parent's Signature _____

Choose one activity. When it is completed, have your child write his or her reaction to the experience at the bottom of the page. Return this page on the last school day of August.

1. Quickie Snack Mix

Make this easy snack to take along with you on a camping trip or a park outing. Mix the following ingredients in a large bowl:

> 4 cups Chex cereal
>
> 1 cup Cheerios
>
> 1 cup peanuts
>
> 1 cup raisins
>
> 1 cup pretzels

Store the snack in an airtight container.

2. Summer Memories Book

Gather photos, souvenirs, travel tickets, postcards, letters, and other items from your summer vacation. Arrange the items in a scrapbook or photo album, and label each one. Include drawings or stories of your favorite summer memories in the book.

Tell about the activity you chose. What did you like about it?

_____

_____

_____

Parent's Signature _____

Choose one activity. When it is completed, have your child write his or her reaction to the experience at the bottom of the page. Return this page on the last school day of the month.

1. Family Night

Plan a "Family Night" in your home. Let everyone in the family choose one short activity (15–30 minutes). For example, your family might choose to do a jigsaw puzzle, eat popcorn while reading stories, listen to music, or look at family photos. Work out a schedule for the activities. Then have fun! Afterwards, have each family member share his or her thoughts and feelings about the night.

2. Family Celebrations Book

Have each family member create a book page showing which holiday or special event he or she has especially enjoyed. Each page should contain a description of the celebration (such as a birthday party or a holiday get-together), along with a sentence telling why the person chose that event. Photos, drawings, family recipes, and other items can be included. When the pages are completed, staple them together to make a book.

Tell about the activity you chose. What did you like about it?

_____

_____

_____

Parent's Signature _____

Across the Curriculum

Real-life learning by its very nature crosses the curriculum. Across the Curriculum homework pages are designed to reinforce classroom learning in language arts, math, science, social studies, art, music, and physical education. These activities offer children the opportunity to successfully follow each task through to completion and to develop the problem-solving skills so important in everyday life.

Each Across the Curriculum page begins with a section informing parents of the purpose of the homework. Easy-to-implement activity directions follow. The activities utilize simple items found in most households.

Before duplicating the homework page, simply fill in the due date. Ask children to bring back each of the completed projects or homework pages by the date you have indicated.

Bowling for Words

Help your child complete this assignment. Turn it in by

_____.

When a child makes words from a set of letters, he or she is learning
- to spell words.
- to see word patterns.
- to use logical reasoning.

Activity

1. Use the letters on the bowling pins to make words.
   Write the words on the lines below.

   _____

   _____

   _____

   _____

   _____

   _____

   _____

2. Count the number of words you wrote.
   Check your bowling score.

   6–10 words — Great!

   11–14 words – Super!

   15–19 words – Wow!

   20 or more words – You're a Bowling Champion!

Parent's Signature _____

Hunt for Proper Nouns

Help your child complete this assignment. Turn it in by _____.

When a child looks for proper nouns and uses them in writing, he or she is learning

- to distinguish parts of speech.
- to practice capitalization skills.
- to write sentences.

Pine School

Kelly

Activity

1. A proper noun names a particular person, place, or thing. For example, *Kelly*, *Alaska*, and *Pine School* are proper nouns. Cut out examples of proper nouns from newspapers or magazines. Glue them in the categories below.

person –   day –

country –   month –

city –   state –

school –   body of water –

2. Write a sentence using the proper nouns you found. Use as many as you can. Don't forget that proper nouns begin with a capital letter!

_____

_____

_____

Parent's Signature _____

47

What a Story!

Help your child complete this assignment. Turn it in by _____.

When a child completes a story frame, he or she is learning
- to think creatively.
- to apply rules of grammar.
- to complete sentences appropriately.

Activity

1. Complete the story below by filling in the blanks with interesting words or phrases.

On my way home from _____, a _____ appeared in

front of me. I couldn't believe my eyes! It had a _____ and it

_____. I felt brave and went close to it. I held out a

_____ and touched it. I was surprised because it felt

_____. Suddenly there was a _____ and I had

to close my eyes. When I opened them again, I saw _____

_____. I ran and ran. When I got home, the first thing I did was

_____.

2. Draw a picture of the story on the back of this paper.
3. Read the story to someone at home.
4. Bring this paper to school and share your story with the class.

Parent's Signature _____

Compound Words Match-Up

Help your child complete this assignment. Turn it in by _____.

When a child plays a memory game with compound words, he or she is learning

- to identify words that form compound words.
- to develop memory skills.
- to plan problem-solving strategies.

Activity

1. Cut 20 cards from medium-weight paper or use 20 index cards.

2. With your family, make a list of ten compound words. Try to use word parts that cannot be used more than once in your game. For example, do not include *sometime* and *anyone* because both *some* and *any* can be combined with *time* and *one*.

3. Write *A* on ten of the cards. Then turn them over. On each *A* card write a word that comes first in the compound words. For example, for *rainbow* write *rain* and for *sunshine*, write *sun*.

4. Label the remaining cards *B*. Then turn these over, and write on them the words that come second in each compound.

5. Shuffle the cards and lay them facedown on a table. Then take turns turning over a pair of *A* and *B* cards. If the two cards form a compound word, the player keeps them and takes another turn. If they do not, he or she returns them facedown to their original positions and the next person gets a turn.

6. Keep playing until all the cards have been picked up. The player with the most cards wins.

Tell about the activity. What did you like about it?

_____

_____

Parent's Signature _____

Comic Creations

Help your child complete this assignment. Turn it in by _____.

When a child rewrites a comic strip, he or she is learning

- to create dialogue.
- to use capitalization and punctuation skills.
- to write sentences to match illustrations.

Activity

1. Cut out a comic strip from the newspaper. If possible, use the comic strips found in the Sunday paper because these are larger and easier to work with.

2. Cover the speech balloons by gluing white paper over them.

3. Write sentences in the balloons to create your own dialogue for the comic strip.

4. Read the comic strip to someone at home.

5. Bring your comic strip to school and share it with the class.

Parent's Signature _____

More Than One Meaning

Help your child complete this assignment. Turn it in by_____.

When a child looks up words in the dictionary and checks their various meanings, he or she is learning

- to use the dictionary.
- to identify words with multiple meanings.
- to distinguish the different meanings of words.

Activity

1. Think of three to five words that name different parts of the body and that have other meanings as well. For example, *foot* can mean the end part of a leg or a length equaling 12 inches.

2. Check the various meanings of the words you chose by looking them up in a dictionary.

3. On a sheet of paper, write two definitions for each word. Then write two sentences illustrating the different meanings.

   Examples: I hopped on one <u>foot</u>.

   This rope is one <u>foot</u> long.

4. Bring your paper to school.

Parent's Signature _____

A Lantern Poem

Help your child complete this assignment. Turn it in by _____.

When a child writes a descriptive poem, he or she is learning

- to express thoughts and feelings.
- to observe the world closely.
- to create colorful images with language.

Activity

Wind
Cool, fresh
Rustles leaves
Blows through my hair
Breeze

1. Choose a topic to write about, such as family, sports, or something in nature.
2. Write a lantern poem about the topic. A lantern poem is a five-line poem written in the shape of a Japanese lantern.

   First line: Write a noun that has one syllable.
   Second line: Describe the noun using two syllables.
   Third line: Describe the noun using three syllables.
   Fourth line: Describe the noun using four syllables.
   Fifth line: Write a one-syllable word that has almost the same meaning as the noun.

3. Cut out a lantern shape from colored paper. Copy your poem onto the shape.
4. Tape a loop of yarn to the top of the lantern for hanging.
5. Bring your lantern poem to school and show it to the class.

Parent's Signature _____

Add It Up

Help your child complete this assignment. Turn it in by _____.

When a child plays addition games with cards, he or she is learning

- to practice addition facts.
- to make computations mentally.
- to follow directions.

Activity

1. Get a deck of playing cards. Set aside the kings, queens, and jacks. Shuffle the remaining cards and lay them facedown in a pile.

2. Players decide on a number from 50 to 100.

3. Players take turns drawing one card at a time and laying it faceup in a discard pile. When a player picks up a card, he or she adds the number to the previous numbers drawn and says the sum aloud. For example, if 4 and 5 were already drawn and a player picked up a 6, he or she would call out 15.

4. The game continues until a player picks up a card and reaches a sum that is equal to or greater than the number selected at the beginning of the game.

Tell about the activity.

How many people played? _____

What was your goal number? _____

What did you like about the game?

_____

_____

_____

Parent's Signature _____

Grocery Store Math

Help your child complete this assignment. Turn it in by _____.

When a child solves problems involving the cost of groceries, he or she is learning
- to add prices.
- to make selections based on available money.
- to write and solve word problems.

Activity

Look through a grocery store flyer.

Solve the following problems.

1. Suppose you had $10.00. Make a grocery list totaling as close to $10.00 as you can without going over. List the items, their prices, and the total cost.

   _____

   _____

   _____

   _____

   _____

2. List two nonfood items from the flyer. _____

   Add up their prices. _____

   What is the smallest bill you can use to buy them? _____

   What change would you receive? _____

3. Write a word problem using the grocery store flyer. Then solve your problem.

   _____

   _____

   _____

   _____

Parent's Signature _____

Make a Number

Help your child complete this assignment. Turn it in by _____.

When a child plays a number game and forms large numbers, he or she is learning

- to understand place value.
- to make number comparisons.
- to use problem-solving strategies.

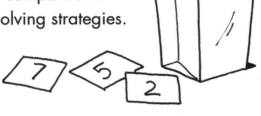

Activity

1. Write the numbers *1* to *9* on index cards. Put the cards in a lunch bag.
2. Each player draws three short lines on a sheet of paper. The lines stand for a three-digit number.
3. The first player chooses a card from the bag and shows it to the other players. Each player writes the number on one of the lines on his or her paper.
4. The game continues with players taking turns drawing a card from the bag. Each time, players look at the number selected and write it on one of their empty lines.
5. After three cards have been drawn, the players look at their papers and say the number they formed. The player who has the highest number wins the round.
6. Put the cards back in the bag to play the next round. Play at least five rounds.

Variations:

- The player with the lowest number wins the round.
- Draw four lines on the paper and select four cards to make a four-digit number.
- Pick a number before play begins. Try to get as close to that number as you can.

Describe your strategy for playing this game. Did it always work?

_____

_____

_____

Parent's Signature _____

How Old Are the Books?

Help your child complete this assignment. Turn it in by _____.

When a child calculates a book's age and records it on a chart, he or she is learning

- to use computation skills.
- to look for copyright information.
- to use a chart.

Activity

1. Find six books that have different copyright dates. The date is usually found on the inside cover of the book.

2. List each title and its publication date on the chart below.

Title of Book	Copyright Date	Book's Age

3. Calculate the age of each book. Fill in the ages on the chart.

4. Look at your chart. What is the oldest copyright date? _____ What is the latest copyright date? _____

5. On the back of this page, explain how you discovered the book's age.

Parent's Signature _____

Guess and Measure

Help your child complete this assignment. Turn it in by _____.

When a child estimates and measures length, he or she is learning

- to make close estimates.
- to make comparisons.
- to measure accurately.

Activity

Estimate the answer to each question. Then measure with a ruler to check your guess.

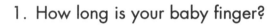

1. How long is your baby finger?

2. What is the diameter of a quarter?

3. How thick is your front door?

4. What is the length of a spoon?

5. Spread out your hand. How far is it from the tip of your thumb to the tip of your baby finger?

6. Choose an object in your house. Estimate its length and then check your guess.

   _____.
   (object)

	Estimate	Measurement
1.		
2.		
3.		
4.		
5.		
6.		

Think about the activity. Did your guesses get more accurate each time? Why or why not?

_____

_____

_____

Parent's Signature _____

TV Watch

Help your child complete this assignment. Turn it in by _____.

When a child records information on a graph, he or she is learning

- to collect data.
- to tabulate and record results.
- to make comparisons.

Activity

1. Keep track of how many hours of TV you watch every
   day for a week. Record your findings on a sheet of paper.

2. Make a bar graph showing how much TV you watched each day.
   Label the graph and give it a title.

3. Look at the graph and answer these questions.

- On which day did you watch the most TV ? _____
  How many hours of TV did you watch that day? _____

- On which day did you watch the least TV? _____
  How many hours of TV did you watch that day? _____

- What is the total number of hours you watched TV that week? _____

4. Bring your graph to school. Compare your results with those of your classmates.

Parent's Signature _____

Making Boxes

Help your child complete this assignment. Turn it in by _____.

When a child plays a strategy game, he or she is learning

- to apply logic.
- to use trial and error.
- to solve problems.

Activity

Play this game with a partner.

1. Draw a grid of dots on a sheet of paper. Choose between 3 and 7 for the number of rows and columns you'll make.

2. Take turns connecting two dots at a time with a line. You may draw lines across and down but not diagonally.

3. Whenever a player draws a line to form a box, the player claims the box by writing his or her initial in it.

4. If a player draws a line and forms two boxes, the player claims both boxes.

5. The game continues until all the dots have been connected. The player with the most boxes wins.

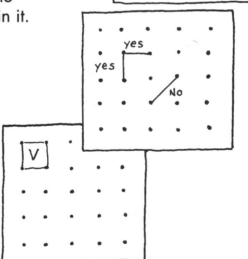

Describe your game strategy.

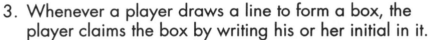

_____

_____

_____

Parent's Signature _____

Breathing Rates

Help your child complete this assignment. Turn it in by _____.

When a child compares breathing rates, he or she is learning

- to gather data.
- to observe how the human body works.
- to form conclusions.

Activity

Do you think everyone breathes at the same rate?
Find out with this activity.

1. Ask an adult in the family to be the timer. Have your
    family members sit quietly and count their breaths for
    30 seconds. (One inhale and one exhale count as
    one breath.)

2. Record each person's name and number of breaths on the lines below.
    Then multiply each number by 2 to get the breathing rate per minute.

Name	Number of Breaths in 30 Seconds	Breathing Rate per Minute
_____	_____	_____
_____	_____	_____
_____	_____	_____
_____	_____	_____
_____	_____	_____
_____	_____	_____

3. Did everyone have the same breathing rate? _____
    Explain _____

4. What do you think happens to the breathing rate when you exercise hard?

    _____

    How could you check your answer? _____

    _____

    Try it.

    Parent's Signature _____

Blown by Wind

Help your child complete this assignment. Turn it in by _____.

When a child observes the effects of wind on soil, he or she is learning

- to see what forces affect the earth's landscape.
- to understand the effects of erosion on people and the environment.
- to understand the importance of conservation.

Activity

The surface of the earth is constantly being changed by different forces. Find out one way in which wind affects the earth's surface when you do this activity.

1. Working outside, scoop some dirt into a pie plate to make a "hill." Lay the plate on the ground. Blow at the dirt through a straw. What happens?

   _____

   _____

2. Rebuild the hill. Put some craft sticks, straws, or twigs into the dirt to represent trees. Blow at the dirt again through the straw. What happens?

   _____

   _____

3. Which hill lost its dirt faster? Why do you think this happened?

   _____

   _____

4. When soil is lifted and blown away, it is called erosion. Why do you think farmers have to be concerned about soil erosion?

   _____

   _____

5. What is one way that farmers can reduce soil erosion?

   _____

   _____

Extension: Water is another force that can erode soil. On the back of this paper, write an experiment that would show how water affects soil erosion.

Parent's Signature _____

Test for Fat

Help your child complete this assignment. Turn it in by _____.

When a child tests foods for fat, he or she is learning
- to confirm the presence of fat.
- to draw conclusions.
- to conduct an experiment.

milk	⟍⟍⟍
butter	⟍⟍⟍
apple	⟍⟍⟍

Activity

This activity will show you which foods contain fat.

1. Divide a sheet of paper into nine sections. In each section, write the name of a food you want to test. Here are some you might want to use: butter, milk, fruit juice, peanut butter, apple, cheese, potato chip, celery.

2. Make a spot in each section by rubbing the food onto the paper. For milk and other messy items, dip a cotton swab into the food and then "paint" a spot on the paper.

3. Wait until the spot is dry. Then check the paper. A dry spot means that the food has no fat. A greasy spot means that the food contains fat.

4. Which foods had fat?_____

_____

_____

Parent's Signature _____

A Sliding Race

Help your child complete this assignment. Turn it in by _____.

When a child sets up a race to see which objects slide fastest, he or she is learning

- to explore the concept of friction.
- to see that the amount of friction can vary.
- to study test results.

Activity

When two surfaces rub against each other, a force called friction makes it harder for them to move. In this activity, you will see friction in action!

1. Place an eraser and a paper clip along the edge of a smooth wooden cutting board. Slowly tilt the board.

2. Which object begins moving first? _____

   Which one reaches the bottom of the board first? _____

   Which object creates the most friction when it is rubbed against the board?

   _____

3. Set up a race with three other flat objects. List them below. Write *1*, *2*, and *3* to show the results of the race.

Object	Finished the Race
_____	_____
_____	_____
_____	_____

4. Which object generates the most friction? _____

   Which one generates the least friction? _____

Parent's Signature _____

Search the Yellow Pages

Help your child complete this assignment. Turn it in by _10/31/00_ .

When a child looks for information in the Yellow Pages, he or she is learning

- to group businesses by category.
- to use alphabetizing skills.
- to learn about community resources.

Activity

The Yellow Pages list businesses by category. When you need to find a business, you must look it up under its general category. For example, a place that sells doghouses might be listed under "Pet Shops." Look in the Yellow Pages of your phone book and answer the following questions:

1. How many bowling lanes are listed in your Yellow Pages?

   _____

2. What is the name of a school that teaches you how to drive?

   _____

3. Who could you call to clean your carpets?

   _____

4. What company could give you information about computers?

   _____

5. Where could you go at lunchtime for pizza?

   _____

6. Who could you call about a plumbing problem?

   _____

7. What is the name of a local bookstore?

   _____

Parent's Signature _____

Local Landmarks

Help your child complete this assignment. Turn it in by _____.

When a child draws a grid showing local landmarks, he or she is learning
- to identify directions.
- to identify landmarks in his or her community.
- to note the relative positions of places.

Activity

Make a grid showing various landmarks that are near your home.

1. Divide a sheet of paper into nine sections. Draw your home in the middle square and label it.

2. Label the other squares as shown in the diagram.

3. Fill in the squares with the names of landmarks that are near your home; for example, a friend's home, a park, or a store. List each landmark in the square that shows its position in relation to your home.

4. Bring your grid to school and compare it to your classmates'.

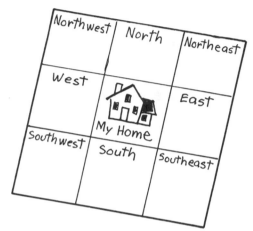

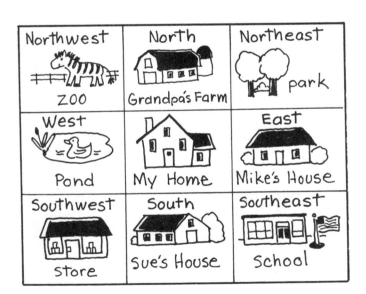

Parent's Signature _____

A Career Survey

Help your child complete this assignment. Turn it in by _____.

When a child conducts an interview and writes a report, he or she is learning

- to formulate questions.
- to listen carefully to responses.
- to organize information.

Activity

1. Interview a family member or a neighbor about his or her job. Prepare for the interview by writing your questions ahead of time. Here are some questions you might want to ask.
   - What hours do you work?
   - Do you need special training for your work?
   - What are your main responsibilities?
   - What kind of qualities or interests should a person have to do your job well?
2. After the interview, write a short report to share with your class.
3. Write a note thanking the person for giving you the interview.

Parent's Signature _____

Made in the U.S.A.

Help your child complete this assignment. Turn it in by _____.

When a child investigates in which parts of a country certain products are made, he or she is learning

- to be aware that products come from a variety of places.
- to identify states in the U.S.
- to recognize a country's resources.

Activity

1. Read the product labels on food packages, clothing, toys, and other items. List ten products that were made in the United States and the states they come from.

   _____   _____

   _____   _____

   _____   _____

   _____   _____

   _____   _____

2. Draw or trace a simple outline of the United States on a sheet of white paper. Glue the outline in the middle of a larger sheet of colored paper.

3. On a small piece of paper, write the name of one of the products and the state where the product was made. Repeat this step for each of the remaining products.

4. Glue the pieces of paper around the sides of the colored paper. Draw a line from each paper to the matching area on the map.

5. Share your project with your family and friends.

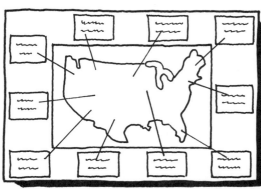

Parent's Signature _____

Lines in Motion

Help your child complete this assignment. Turn it in by _____.

When a child makes a cut-paper design using various kinds of lines, he or she is learning

- to see that lines can show movement.
- to recognize that lines define shapes.
- to experiment with lines.

Activity

1. On a sheet of construction paper, draw a line from the top left corner to the bottom right corner. Make the line "move" by drawing it curved or jagged.
2. Cut on the line to divide the paper into two pieces.
3. Glue one-half of the paper on a contrasting color of paper.
4. Repeat the activity as many times as you like. Experiment with different kinds of lines.

Parent's Signature _____

Split a Shape

Help your child complete this assignment. Turn it in by _____.

When a child creates a design by splitting a shape, he or she is learning

- to be aware of positive and negative space.
- to experiment with lines and shapes.
- to see that the space around a shape contributes to a design.

Activity

1. Cut a geometric shape (such as a circle or square) from colored paper.

2. Draw a line across the shape. The line can be straight, curved, or jagged.

3. Cut along the line to split the shape into two pieces.

4. Glue the pieces back together on a sheet of white paper, but leave a small space where the pieces should connect.

5. How does the split shape look different from the original?

   _____

   _____

6. Repeat the activity as many times as you like. Experiment with the type of line, the number of lines, and the kinds of shapes you use.

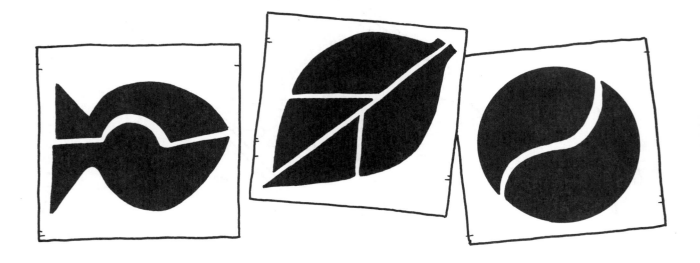

Parent's Signature _____

Magazine Mosaic

Help your child complete this assignment. Turn it in by _____.

When a child makes a mosaic from paper squares, he or she is learning
- to create new shapes from smaller shapes.
- to experiment with color.
- to think creatively.

Activity

1. Think of a picture or design to make. Sketch it lightly on a sheet of drawing paper.
2. Look in magazines for colors to use in your artwork. Cut out small squares from the colors.
3. Glue the squares on the drawing paper to form your picture.
4. With a felt marker and a ruler, draw a border around the paper.
5. Bring your picture to school and share it with the class.

Parent's Signature _____

Musical Glasses

Help your child complete this assignment. Turn it in by _____.

When a child creates music from drinking glasses, he or she is learning

- to experiment with sound.
- to be creative in musical expression.
- to compose and perform music.

Activity

1. Get six to eight tall, clear glasses. Fill them with different amounts of water.

2. Arrange the glasses in a line, beginning with the one with the most water and ending with the glass with the least water.

3. Tap a pencil gently against the top of each glass. Listen to the sound made. Adjust the sound by adding or subtracting water from the glass. Is the sound higher or lower when there is more water in the glass?

   _____

4. Attach pieces of masking tape to the glasses. Number the glasses with a pen.

5. Compose a piece of music with your glasses. Write which glasses to play by writing their numbers on a sheet of paper.

6. Perform your musical piece for your family.

7. Bring your "sheet of music" to school.

Parent's Signature _____

Kinds of Music

Help your child complete this assignment. Turn it in by _____.
When a child listens to various kinds of music, he or she is learning

- to recognize that music comes in many distinct forms.
- to identify different kinds of music.
- to appreciate various types of music.

Activity

There are many kinds of music. Some are easy to hum to and others are not. Some have a certain kind of beat. In this activity, you'll get a chance to listen to different kinds of music and decide what you like or don't like about them.

1. Listen to at least four different kinds of music. You may listen to your family's music collection or listen to the radio or TV. You may also borrow recordings from the library.

2. Look at the list below. Check off the kind of music you listened to.

___ Classical   ___ Folk   ___ Music from Movies

___ Country   ___ Hymn   ___ Opera

___ Disco   ___ Jazz   ___ Pop

Other _____   ___ Rhythm and Blues   ___ Rock and Roll

3. Which kind of music did you like the best? Why?

_____

_____

4. Which kind of music did you like the least? Why?

_____

_____

Parent's Signature _____

Musical Instruments

Help your child complete this assignment. Turn it in by _____.

When a child tries to identify types of musical instruments, he or she is learning
- to distinguish sounds.
- to recognize that instruments belong to certain groups.
- to be aware of the variety of instruments used to produce a musical piece.

Activity

1. Look up musical instruments in an encyclopedia or a library book.
   Find these groups of instruments:
   - Stringed instruments (includes the guitar and violin)
   - Woodwind instruments (includes the flute and saxophone)
   - Brass instruments (includes the trumpet and trombone)
   - Percussion instruments (includes the drum and tambourine)
   - Keyboard instruments (includes the piano and organ)

2. Talk about how the instruments in each group are similar.

3. With your family, select a musical recording. See if you can identify groups of instruments or specific instruments.

4. Which group of instruments did you hear the most?

   _____

5. Which group of instruments do you like the best? Why?

   _____

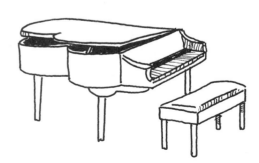

Parent's Signature _____

Knock 'Em Down

Help your child complete this assignment. Turn it in by _____.

When a child tries to knock down targets with a ball, he or she is learning

- to aim accurately.
- to develop large-muscle control.
- to participate in friendly competition.

Activity

1. Get two clean two-liter plastic soda bottles. Peel off the labels.
2. Decorate the bottles with stickers or permanent markers.
3. Set the bottles on a table or a large box outdoors.
4. Have your family members stand a few feet away from the bottles. Then take turns trying to knock the bottles down with a ball. Players get two throws at a time.
5. Play several rounds. If you like, make the game harder by standing farther away from the pins.

Parent's Signature _____

Balloon Toss

Help your child complete this assignment. Turn it in by _____.

When a child bats a balloon back and forth with a partner, he or she is learning

- to keep an eye on a moving target.
- to pass an object to a partner.
- to develop coordination.

Activity

Blow up a balloon and knot its end. Then play catch with a partner. Here are some different ways you can play.

- Decide on a number, such as 20. See if you can bat the balloon back and forth 20 times without letting it fall to the ground.

- Bat the balloon with the hand you do not usually use. For example, if you are right-handed, bat with your left hand. See how long you can keep the ball in the air.

- Use a paper towel tube as a bat. Hit the balloon with the bat and see if your partner can catch it. Then switch roles.

- Use two balloons at a time. Bat your balloons at the same time. See if the two of you can catch the other's balloon.

Tell about the activity. Which way did you like playing the best? Why?

_____

_____

_____

Parent's Signature _____

Freeze!

Help your child complete this assignment. Turn it in by _____.

When a child moves to music and stops at a signal, he or she is learning
- to use a variety of body movements.
- to move to a rhythmic beat.
- to respond to a signal.

Activity

1. Play some lively music on a tape recorder or CD player. One person is *It* and stands by the equipment. The other players move freely around the room. For example, players may walk, dance, hop, or exercise to the music.

2. *It* can stop the music at any time. When that happens, all the other players must "freeze" (stop moving).

3. The last person to freeze becomes *It.*

4. Repeat the activity several times.

Tell about the activity. What did you like about it?

_____

_____

Parent's Signature _____

Fun With Literature

Fun With Literature homework is designed to help stimulate children's interest in books. Each page contains a variety of activities that focus on a specific literature theme and require children to delve into books. As children complete these activities, they will gain an understanding of literature and an appreciation of both fiction and nonfiction books.

The pages in this section may be used independently or they may be included as a supplement to your classroom literature program. Choose the appropriate homework page for students. Then simply fill in the number of activities that must be completed and the due date for turning in the paper before reproducing the page for your class. Of course, many eager learners may want to do all the activities! Encourage students to bring one or more of their favorite projects to school for display or discussion.

A Super Story

Help your child complete this assignment. Turn it in by _____.

A fiction book tells a make-believe story. Choose a fiction book that you have enjoyed. Then complete and check off at least _____ of the following activities.

☐ Make a postcard showing the setting of the story (where the story takes place). On the back, write two or three sentences describing the picture.

☐ Design a new cover for the book. Include the title and author's name, and a picture that represents the book. Add yourself as the illustrator.

☐ Fold a piece of paper in half. Then fold it in half again to make a four-page booklet. Draw pictures showing four main events in the story.

☐ Read your favorite part of the story to a family member.

☐ Advertise the book by creating a TV commercial for it. Act out the commercial for your family.

☐ Write a book review telling why children your age would enjoy the book.

☐ Put on a puppet show based on all or part of the story.

☐ Make a pamphlet that describes the main characters that children will meet in the story.

Parent's Signature _____

What a Character!

Help your child complete this assignment. Turn it in by _____.

Choose an interesting story character. Then complete and check off at least _____ of the following activities.

☐ Draw a picture, make a puppet, or create a clay sculpture to show what the character looks like.

☐ Write the character's name vertically on a sheet of paper. Then use each letter to begin a word, phrase, or sentence that tells about the character or describes what the character did in the story.

☐ Make up a poem about the character. The poem does not have to rhyme.

☐ Suppose this character was your neighbor. Write how you would feel and why.

☐ Make a sketch showing what this character's bedroom might look like. Explain your drawing to a family member.

☐ Write a paragraph telling whether you think this character acts like a real person.

☐ Draw an outline of the character on a sheet of paper. Cut out the outline. At the top, write the character's name. Then add words and phrases describing the character.

☐ Write three questions you would like to ask the author about this character.

Parent's Signature _____

Is That a Fact?

Help your child complete this assignment. Turn it in by _____.

A nonfiction book gives facts about a person, place, or thing. For example, biographies (stories that tell about a person's life), science books, and history books are nonfiction. Choose a nonfiction book you have enjoyed. Then complete and check off at least _____ of the following activities.

☐ Write five facts you learned from the book.

☐ Draw a picture illustrating the main topic of the book.

☐ Make a poster telling why children your age would find the book interesting.

☐ Read a paragraph from the book. Then rewrite it in your own words.

☐ Write seven questions that are answered in the book.

☐ Have someone ask you questions about the book. See if you can answer the questions correctly.

☐ Make a chart listing new words you learned. Write a definition for each word.

☐ Show the book to someone at home. Read an interesting part to a family member.

Parent's Signature _____

Name _____

Fairy Tale Fun

Help your child complete this assignment. Turn it in by _____.

Read a fairy tale. Then complete and check off at least _____ of the following activities.

- ☐ Draw the hero or the heroine. Write three sentences describing that character.
- ☐ Draw the character that is evil or dangerous. Write three sentences describing that character.
- ☐ Write what the hero or heroine's problem is. Tell how the problem gets solved.
- ☐ Imagine that the fairy tale is going to be turned into a movie. Design a movie poster advertising it.
- ☐ Suppose that the fairy tale is going to become a stage play. Write which character you would like to play and why.
- ☐ Make a shoebox diorama showing a scene from the story.
- ☐ Pretend that the fairy tale actually happened and that you are a reporter who has just finished interviewing the hero or heroine. Write a newspaper article describing what happened to that character.

Parent's Signature _____

Poetry Corner

Help your child complete this assignment. Turn it in by _____.

Choose an interesting poem from a poetry book. Then complete and check off at least _____ of the following activities.

☐ Memorize all or part of the poem. Recite the poem to your family.

☐ Write three or more sentences telling why you like the poem.

☐ Copy descriptive words and phrases from the poem on a piece of paper. Use the words to create a new poem.

☐ Close your eyes and have someone read the poem to you. Then draw a picture showing what you "saw" in your mind when you heard the poem.

☐ List all the rhyming words that are used in the poem.

☐ Tape-record yourself reading the poem.

☐ Make up actions or create a dance to fit the poem. Have someone read the poem while you move to the words.

☐ Write the name of the poet. Read a few other poems he or she has written. List the titles of the new poems on the piece of paper.

Parent's Signature _____

Celebrate an Author

Help your child complete this assignment. Turn it in by _____.

Choose an author whose books you like. Then complete and check off at least _____ of the following activities.

☐ Look at the back inside cover of a book jacket and read information about the author. Write three facts you learned.

☐ Make a bookmark listing the books the author has written. If there are too many books to fit on a bookmark, then include only your favorites.

☐ Write a paragraph telling why you would recommend this author's work.

☐ Make a poster showing some of the characters the author has created. Write the characters' names beside their pictures and tell which books they are from.

☐ Write a letter telling the author why you enjoy his or her books. Mail the letter to the book's publisher. Ask a librarian for the publisher's current address.

☐ Make a list of interview questions you would ask the author if you met him/her.

☐ Design an award for the author. On the award, give one reason why this person's work is outstanding. (Example: The author makes her characters come to life or has a knack for telling humorous stories.)

Parent's Signature _____

Literature Scavenger Hunt

Help your child complete this assignment. Turn it in by _____.

Visit your local library and have fun discovering the wonderful world of books! Complete and check off at least _____ of the following activities.

☐ Find a book about the life of a famous person. Write the title and the author's name.
_____

☐ Find a book that is written and illustrated by the same person. Write the title and author's name. _____

☐ Find a book that has beautiful pictures. Write the title and the illustrator's name.
_____

☐ Find a book that shows you how to do something. Write its title.
_____

☐ Find a book that has photographs. Write its title.
_____

☐ Find a book that describes what life was like more than 100 years ago. Write its title.
_____

☐ Find a book that tells a story in rhyme. Write the title and the author's name.
_____

☐ Find a book that tells about a country. Write the title.
_____

Parent's Signature _____

Family Adventures

A trip to the grocery store . . . or a trip to the park? Family Adventure homework pages invite students and their families to go on real-life or make-
believe adventures together. And naturally, families learn as they go! These
real-life experiences will develop creative and critical-thinking skills as well
as enhance learning in social studies, reading, writing, and
science.

Each homework page begins with an idea for an adventure. There is always
the possibility of turning a real-life adventure into a make-believe one if the
family is unable to go by saying "Let's pretend we went to . . ."

When assigning a Family Adventure, fill in the due date at the top of the
page and write the number of activities to be completed before duplicating
the page for each child. Discuss the page with the class and then send it
home. Families discuss the activities and choose the ones they want to do. As
each activity is completed, the corresponding box is checked off. Children
return the page to school by the due date.

Neighborhood Adventure

Help your child complete this assignment. Turn it in by _____.

Take a walk with your family around the neighborhood. Complete and check off at least ____ of the following activities. Have fun!

☐ Write two house numbers from your street. Find their sum.

☐ List three nonliving things and three living things you see.

☐ Keep track of the number of red vehicles that pass by as you walk.

☐ List six things found in nature and six things made by people.

☐ Count the number of homes that have chimneys.

☐ Take a plastic bag with you. Collect three interesting things from your walk.

☐ Write the sounds you hear.

☐ See how far 100 steps take you.

☐ Write the time you left home and the time you returned. Figure out how long you were gone on your walk.

☐ Find out the names of at least two kinds of trees or shrubs.

Parent's Signature _____

Grocery Store Adventure

Help your child complete this assignment. Turn it in by _____.

Go to the grocery store with your family. Complete and check off at least _____ of the following activities. Good luck!

☐ Look for ten fruits and vegetables. Write their names in alphabetical order.

☐ Add up the prices of three snack foods.

☐ List three foods you've never eaten before.

☐ Find five things that are measured in fluid ounces.

☐ Weigh an orange. Then weigh a grapefruit. Calculate the difference.

☐ List seven nonfood items you can buy.

☐ Find something on sale. Figure out the difference between the sale price and the regular price.

☐ Write the names of four companies that produce canned foods.

☐ List eight foods that must be kept frozen.

☐ Find six items that come from other countries.

Parent's Signature _____

87

Library Adventure

Help your child complete this assignment. Turn it in by _____.

Plan a day when the family can visit the public library together. Complete and check off at least _____ of the following activities.

☐ List the different kinds of materials you can borrow from the library.

☐ Ask the librarian when the children's section is usually the most crowded. Find out why.

☐ Ask how many books can be checked out at one time and for how long.

☐ Find out the names of other library branches in your area. List them.

☐ Describe one display you see.

☐ Write what you could do to find out where children's science books are shelved.

☐ Go to the children's section. Describe what has been done to make that section appealing to children.

☐ Go to the Reference Books section. The books here may be looked at but not borrowed. Write the name of an interesting book you find.

☐ Write down the library's hours. Figure out what time you think is the best for you to visit the library regularly.

Parent's Signature _____

Restaurant Adventure

Help your child complete this assignment. Turn it in by _____.

Spend time with your family at a favorite restaurant. Take a piece of paper and a pencil to write down information you will need to do the activities. Complete and check off at least _____ of the following activities. Happy eating!

☐ Look at the menu. Point to three foods you've never tasted.

☐ Write down the prices of the most expensive and the least expensive items. Figure out the difference.

☐ Count how many items on the menu cost less than $5.00.

☐ Find out how many customers can be seated at one time. How many people are there now?

☐ Count the tables in the restaurant. If there were four people sitting at each table, how many people would there be in all?

☐ Suppose you can't eat any animal products. Name two foods you could choose from the menu.

☐ Find out when the restaurant closes. Write how long you have until closing time.

☐ After everyone in your family has ordered, estimate the bill. See how close your guess was when the bill arrives.

☐ Sketch a map showing the route your family takes to get from your home to the restaurant.

☐ Go outside and look at the area around the restaurant. Check the phrase that best describes the restaurant's location:

___ residential
___ city center
___ shopping mall
___ business/industrial
___ countryside
other _____

Parent's Signature _____

Park Adventure

Help your child complete this assignment. Turn it in by_____.

Enjoy a day at the park with your family. Make the time there a fun learning experience. Complete and check off at least _____ of the following activities.

☐ Make a list of five things children can do at the park.

☐ Write the names of the streets that border the park.

☐ Look for the following items. Check off the ones you see:

__ swing   __ sand   __ picnic table
__ slide   __ water fountain   __ climbing equipment

☐ Estimate how many children there are at the park.

☐ Point to three places where people could enjoy a picnic.

☐ Draw a map showing a bird's-eye view of the park.

☐ Estimate how long it will take you to walk around the park. Then check your guess.

☐ List the activities you see people doing.

☐ Write what you like best about the park.

☐ Name at least three different types of trees and plants.

Parent's Signature _____

Timely Tips Newsletters

Timely Tips Newsletters are perfect mediums for conveying important information to parents on such topics as homework, reading, television, and self-confidence. Parents want to be good partners in their child's education, but they often lack the knowledge or confidence to deal with these issues in an effective way.

Share and discuss these Timely Tips Newsletters with parents at Open House, or send them home with students at appropriate times throughout the year. You will find that parents will appreciate this valuable support/ assistance.

Homework

Timely Tips Newsletter

Did You Know?

Homework can turn into "homeplay" when you support your child and do your best to make learning at home a fun experience. Use the following tips to help your child make the most of homework experiences.

- Set a regular time and place to do the homework. Allow your child to participate in the decision-making process.

- Help your child find a quiet and comfortable place to work. Encourage him or her to avoid interruptions. Turn off the TV.

- Provide the necessary tools, such as paper, pencils, crayons, and scissors.

- When necessary, read the directions to your child and make sure they are understood.

- If necessary, demonstrate how to complete the homework before having your child try it alone.

- Whenever appropriate, sign your child's homework paper. This sends a message to the teacher that you are involved in your child's learning.

- If you have any questions regarding assignments, ask the teacher.

- Praise your child's efforts and keep the atmosphere positive.

 Cloudy With a Chance of Meatballs

Reading

 Dog in the Deep Dark Woods

Timely Tips Newsletter

Did You Know?

Your child will become a better learner when you are his or her partner in education. As one of the most important people in your child's life, you have an opportunity to make a critical difference in how successful your child will be in school. Reading together is one way to become your child's partner in education. Use the following tips to foster your child's love of reading at home.

- Set time aside each night when you and your child can enjoy reading together. Let your child read to you or take turns reading passages aloud.

- Serve as a role model by letting your child see that you like to read books, magazines, and other materials. If possible, share what you've read with your child if the topics are interesting and appropriate.

- Remember not to turn every reading session into a lesson. Your overall goal is to provide a pleasurable reading experience.

- Show interest in what your child is reading. Ask questions and make comments that will let your child know you are curious about the book. For example:
  * What do you think will happen next?
  * I didn't read the first part of the book. Can you tell me what happened?
  * The main character has a problem. What would you do if you were the character?
  * Do you think the problem will be solved in the next chapter? Let's find out.

- When your child finishes a story, ask if he or she liked the way it ended. If not, ask how the ending might be changed.

- Visit the library often and help your child choose books that are the appropriate level. The children's librarian can direct you to popular topics and authors.

- If your child does not have a library card, help him/her fill out an application for one. Give your child the responsibility of signing out books.

 # Television

Timely Tips Newsletter

Did You Know?

As every parent knows, television can interfere with and delay the completion of homework and limit social interactions and physical fitness. Use the following techniques to make television-viewing a more meaningful experience for your child.

- Set limits. Establish good habits by allowing your child to view TV for only an hour (or less) a day.

- Plan. Look at your local television guide and decide together which shows to watch. Talk about which ones are appropriate and at what times they should be viewed.

- Participate. Watch together the shows you choose. Discuss parts of the show and explain things when necessary. Ask your child for ideas about ways the show could have been presented differently.

- Monitor. Encourage your child to choose programs about positive and loving situations. Discuss the characters and why they do what they do.

- Analyze commercials. Help your child analyze commercials and recognize exaggerated claims.

- Seek alternatives. Instead of watching television, have your child participate in activities such as music lessons; after-school sports, programs or clubs; or at-home arts and crafts projects.

Learning on the Go

Timely Tips Newsletter

Did You Know?

The real world is the most natural place for your child to learn. It abounds with new and exciting educational experiences. Invite your child to learn in the real world by participating with you in some of the following activities.

- Visit community buildings and attractions, such as a farm, museum, or fire station.

- Take your child on errands to the grocery store, cleaners, post office, and hardware store. Take time to browse around and talk about the different jobs people have.

- Provide free or unstructured time. Invite your child to listen to music, daydream, or learn to entertain him- or herself.

- Take a train trip or a bus ride.

- Have your child obtain a library card and visit the library regularly. Set a good example for your child by checking out books for yourself as well.

- Take walks in your neighborhood.

- Go to special events, such as sporting events, concerts, or movies. Try to find events that are free and age-appropriate.

- Encourage your child to join community organizations, such as the Scouts, 4-H Club, Camp Fire, soccer, or T-ball programs.

- Play a board game or do a puzzle together.

- Read signs, license plates, bumper stickers, and billboards together.

- Talk about the environment, such as the colors, smells, and noises around you.

- When in the car, talk about directions, traffic rules, and what to expect next.

Building Your Child's Self-Confidence

Timely Tips Newsletter

Did You Know?

With support and guidance, every child can learn. And you can provide that support by working to build your child's self-confidence in learning. Use the following tips to help your child develop self-esteem and self-confidence.

- Praise your child every time you see something positive. Be specific about your praise by telling him or her what you like and why.

- Set realistic goals for your child.

- Be patient when your child tries something new. Remind your child that "practice makes perfect."

- Let your child learn things on his or her own whenever possible. Children spend a lot of time trying to make sense of their world.

- Display your child's creations, such as drawings, paintings, and writings.

- Photograph your child engaged in a learning task and display the photos around the house.

- Encourage your child in a positive way to try again when he or she is unsuccessful or frustrated.

- Spend time together. Work, play, talk, or just be together for a little while every day.

- Through words and hugs, let your child know that you believe in him or her.

- Remind your child that it is okay to make mistakes.